The Financial Advisor's Guide to Building Trust

How Financial Professionals Grow Relationships, Referrals, and Revenue—One Memorable Event at a Time

by Michael Oana

The Financial Advisor's Guide to Building Trust by Michael Oana

ISBN: 979-8-218-86452-1
Copyright © 2026 by Michael Oana

Cover design by Reality Coaching for Writers
Interior design by atritex.com

Available in print from your local bookstore, online, or from the publisher.

For more information on this book and the author visit: michaeloana.com

All rights reserved. Non-commercial interests may reproduce portions of this book without the express written permission, provided the text does not exceed 500 words. When reproducing text from this book, include the following credit line: "*The Financial Advisor's Guide to Building Trust* by Michael Oana."

Commercial interests: No part of this publication may be reproduced in any form, stored in a retrieval system, or transmitted in any form by any means—electronic, photocopy, recording, or otherwise—without prior written permission of the publisher, except as provided by the United States of America copyright law.

Library of Congress Cataloging-in-Publication Data

Oana, Michael.

The Financial Advisor's Guide to Building Trust / Michael Oana, 1st ed.

Printed in the United States of America

This publication is intended for informational purposes only and does not constitute investment advice, a recommendation, or an offer to buy or sell any securities. The scenarios, examples, and client stories presented throughout this guide are for illustrative purposes and should not be interpreted as guarantees of future results. Any references to financial strategies, products, or services are general in nature and may not be suitable for all investors. Readers should consult with a qualified financial professional to determine the appropriateness of any strategy or product based on their individual circumstances. This material is not intended to replace your firm's compliance policies or procedures. Financial professionals are encouraged to consult their firm's compliance department before implementing any marketing or client engagement strategies described herein. Michael Oana Retirement Planning Specialist is an independent company. Securities offered through Cetera Wealth Services, LLC, member FINRA/SIPC. Advisory Services offered through Cetera Investment Advisors LLC, a registered investment advisor. Cetera is under separate ownership from any other named entity.

Praise for...

"This is a field guide for advisors who want steady, durable growth. Michael shows exactly how he built a credible brand and loyal client base through consistent action and authentic connection, then turns it into a repeatable system. I've seen his approach up close through FMG; now you can put it to work in your firm."
— Susan Theder, Chief Marketing and Experience Officer, FMG Marketing

"Memorable events create memorable advisors and memorable advisors get more introductions. Advisors who want to increase referrals without begging for them must read this guide. Michael demonstrates how strategic client events create emotional engagement, deepen loyalty, and open the door to personal introductions. This is relationship marketing at its best: systematic, memorable, and highly referable."
— Bill Cates, CSP, CPAE, author of *The Language of Referrals* and *Radical Relevance*

"Michael reminds us that being a great advisor isn't just about managing portfolios—it's about creating meaningful connections and lasting value. This book captures the heart of what makes clients stay: trust, care, and genuine relationships."

—Pete Bush, CFP®, CEPA, Financial Advisor, Horizon Financial Group

"In *Building Trust*, veteran author Michael Oana shares practical ways to create unforgettable client events that deepen trust and drive referrals. Blending insight, warmth, and real-world examples, Oana helps advisors stand out by focusing on connection over conversion—and turning every event into a story clients love to tell."

—Peter Montoya, author of *The Brand Called You*

"Michael illustrates how thoughtfully crafted client experiences go beyond hospitality to become a strategic engine for trust, loyalty, and referrals. What resonated most for me, as a marketing leader, is how naturally his approach aligns with core marketing disciplines: understanding your audience, shaping authentic moments that reinforce your brand, and building a repeatable system that deepens engagement over time. His frameworks turn events into relationship capital and provide a clear, scalable path for advisors looking to grow through meaningful, memorable client interactions. This is practical, human, and genuinely differentiated."

—Ladan Massir, Senior Managing Director, Head of Advisor and Financial Institution Growth Marketing, Non-registered associate, Cetera

"Michael Oana has been part of the Summit / Cetera family for 20 years. He and his team are well known for their outstanding client service and incredible events. He has been part of our Circle of Excellence for 20 years in a row."
—Marshall T. Leeds, President & CEO, Regional Director, Summit Financial Networks

(The Cetera Financial Group's Circle of Excellence recognition is not a guarantee of future investment success and should not be construed as an endorsement of by any client.)

"Trust gets built in rooms, over meals, through shared experiences. Michael has spent 30 years mastering that craft. This book hands you the blueprint."
—Drew Keever, Co-founder, Advisor Finder

These testimonials were given by individuals who are not clients of the financial advisor, and no compensation was provided directly or indirectly. These testimonials are not a guarantee of future performance or investment success, and the testimonials may not be representative of the experience of other customers. Please visit BrokerCheck (https://brokercheck.finra.org) to see more on the background of this professional.

Table of Contents

Acknowledgements ix

Introduction: Why Entertainment Works When Numbers Don't xi
- Set up the core argument: trust is built socially, not through spreadsheets. Why client events lead to retention, referrals, and revenue

Chapter 1: The Relationship Business 1
- Why numbers alone won't make you a top advisor
- Personal story of Michael's early career
- Case for client appreciation as a marketing strategy

Chapter 2: Build Your Brand Through Experience 9
- Define your firm's event personality
- Align your client base with your entertainment style
- Use venues and vendors that elevate your brand
- Tips from Disney, Ritz, and Chick-fil-A

Chapter 3: Planning Memorable Events 17
- Types of events: educational, social, hybrid
- Sample calendar with seasonal themes
- How to manage budgets of all sizes
- Event checklists and planning templates

Chapter 4: The Execution Edge 27
- First impressions
- Hosting tips: timing, flow, energy
- Sample scripts, signage, and toasts
- Hospitality secrets that make people feel known

Chapter 5: Follow-Up That Converts 35
- Why the fortune is in the follow-up
- What to say after the event
- Referral ask scripts
- Building your drip system and CRM pipeline

Chapter 6: Failures, Flops, and Fixes 43
- What to do when events go sideways
- Real stories of botched venues, busted budgets, and blunders
- How to recover with grace—and gain trust in the process

Chapter 7: Scaling Your Strategy 49
- Bringing in referral partners and sponsors
- How to train staff and systematize the client experience
- Building buzz through social media
- When and how to go virtual

Appendix 57

Acknowledgements

I'd like to thank the University of South Carolina Moore School of Business for a great education and foundation. I'm also grateful for my internship at Walt Disney World and for Dick Nunis, then President of Walt Disney Attractions, who took time out of his busy day to meet with me.

I'm thankful for Spring Valley Country Club, here in Columbia, for hiring me as I wrapped up my time at the university. Early in my career, I had the opportunity to work with one of the largest investment firms in the world, and I loved the work we did there.

I'm especially grateful for my friends within Summit Financial Networks, a part of Cetera. For more than 20 years, that partnership has helped make change both possible and fun. I've learned so much from those colleagues, and they've shaped the way I entertain, serve, and think about client events.

When I started, I was in my early twenties, still learning and finding my way. Along the journey I've had great mentors. One of them, Coach Cathy Townsend, encouraged me to put what I've learned into this "recipe." She has been my professional and life coach for more than 20 years, and I'm humbled and blessed by her guidance.

Introduction

Why Entertainment Works When Numbers Don't

In any given neighborhood, on any given Tuesday, there's someone sitting at their kitchen table, bills stacked to one side, a browser tab open to an article called "How to Retire Before 50." That person won't call a financial advisor. Not today. Probably not ever.

> "You don't sell money. You sell clarity."

You're not surprised. Many Americans never seek financial advice. They're too busy raising kids, working jobs, juggling life.

At first, that statistic sounds troubling. But the more you think about it, the more it starts to make sense. Financial planning is one of the few areas in life where the consequences of doing nothing are invisible—until they're not.

Not every client will take your advice, but it's the ones that do that you can help the most.

Consider a client approaching retirement with multiple accounts scattered across several institutions. In situations like this, an advisor might help organize and consolidate those holdings into a coordinated strategy, easing the administrative complexity and allowing for clearer planning decisions.

So the first paradox of being a financial advisor is this: The people who need you most are the ones least likely to pick up the phone. It's not fear or arrogance. It's inertia. Life gets in the way.

Call this a "tipping point" of indifference. The friction of the unknown outweighs the pain of staying unprepared.

But here's where the financial professional pivots. You don't sell money. You sell clarity.

And people don't wake up wanting financial advice—they wake up wanting financial reassurance.

Coaching Without the Whistle

A financial advisor is a coach.

Not the kind who barks plays from the sidelines, embarrasses their child, and gets banned from games. You're the coach who sees what others can't, who believes in the client's goals before they even know they need goals. You're calling plays in the second half before your client has pulled on their jersey. That's the kind of coach who helps clients pursue long-term financial confidence.

Most people are drowning in information. Advice is not the issue. Structure is.

Your role is to help someone with some knowledge and some understanding gain an abundance of wisdom—to take emotion out of the process and make wealth work for the client.

Consider a situation where a client is thinking about cashing in part of their retirement plan to fund home improvements. In a case like this, an advisor might collaborate with the client's CPA to explore alternative strategies—perhaps identifying a more tax-efficient way to finance the project. This kind of proactive planning can help clients make informed decisions while preserving long-term financial goals.

And this is where the real magic of an advisor comes in: you translate complexity into action.

Why People Trust a Face More Than a Firm

> "Talking about money—real money, with all its entanglements of shame, pride, failure, and hope—is one of the most intimate conversations you can have."

There's a moment in every advisor-client relationship when it either clicks—or it doesn't. It has less to do with credentials and more to do with comfort.

Clients look for a financial advisor the way they'd look for a family doctor. Not the slickest website or the biggest office. The one who feels right and knows them. For many, their financial advisor is a couple's counselor, therapist, and the one who holds their hand as they walk through and to the end of their golden years.

That usually means someone from their world. Someone who knows their neighborhood, who's in their kid's school circle, who volunteers at their church or serves on a board with them.

This isn't branding. It's caring for a neighbor.

People don't open up to strangers. And talking about money—real money, with all its entanglements of shame, pride, failure, and hope—is one of the most intimate conversations you can have.

As an advisor, your job is to get to know the client, understand their goals, and help them lay out a vision. This takes time and practice. Not every client is a good fit for your practice. It's like any relationship—it takes time to build trust and rapport. You have to show that you care and understand their goals first, see if it's a good fit, and gain traction and trust.

Imagine meeting a couple who had previously worked with another firm and felt disappointed by the experience. They might arrive guarded—both emotionally and physically. In a situation like this, an advisor could invite them to a client event, then another, gradually helping them connect with others and hear stories. Over time, those initial, cautious conversations might evolve into planning sessions, and eventually into a trusted partnership. For advisors looking to grow their practice, starting in familiar communities—where trust already exists—can be a meaningful first step. In some cases, even opening your home could be the right way to begin.

The Truth About Transparency

There's a strange thing that happens in financial planning.

Clients want help, but they don't want to show their math.

They downplay the debt. They forget to mention the credit card they haven't paid down since, well… ever. They leave out the inheritance they don't want their spouse to know about.

It's like visiting a doctor without confessing the symptoms. And yet… they come in with their checklists, hoping for a miracle, withholding the one piece of information that would change everything.

Your clients will appreciate you the most when they face a life-changing moment. Retirement, divorce, and death are the times when they need your guidance the most—and where your impact can shine.

Here's your role: not to judge the numbers. You normalize them.

That $1.2 million portfolio? You've seen ten like it.

That $12,000 in credit card debt? You've seen two hundred.

You become, in a sense, their financial immune system—unfazed by what you see, focused only on helping the body get stronger. That's wisdom, and the wisdom of a sage is comforting. The doctor who's seen countless stage-four cancers go into remission offers more than medical advice.

They offer hope. That's you. The buffer between unknown and the soon-to-be enjoyed.

Know the Time, Know the Plan

Everything in financial planning comes back to timing.

Is their kid heading to college in two years? Or twenty? Are they five years from retirement or five weeks?

You manage risk—not as a math equation but as a mirror placed in front of your client. How do they feel when the market swings? Do they see opportunity—or feel like they're about to lose their house?

There's no universal answer. Just the right answer for that person, in that season, with those goals.

And that's what makes your work meaningful.

You're not pushing products. You're interpreting life stages and lining up the money to support dreams.

Being a Guide in the Chaos

When people feel overwhelmed, they don't need more data. They need a roadmap.

This is the purpose of your website. Yours might offer articles, videos, resources that meet people where they are.

It's not a sales funnel. It's you reaching out, asking how you can help. When your first introduction to a client begins with, "I've seen this before and I can help," you're halfway to making a friend for life.

It takes time to build a professional level of trust. I can remember an instance where we spoke with a retired manager. : His wife passed from cancer, and he sought help for estate planning.

The value of financial advisory isn't in the spreadsheets. It's in the stories.

And if you want to grow your practice, start collecting the ones that prove what you already know: when people finally pick up the phone, they're calling someone they already know.

And that someone is you.

CHAPTER ONE

The Relationship Business

Early in my career, I thought hosting a Christmas party would be the perfect way to thank clients and make a splash. I invited folks a month ahead of time, rented space, and tried to make it festive. Four people showed up. It was a complete failure. I was embarrassed, but I learned an important lesson: timing and planning matter, especially when people are already overwhelmed with holiday obligations.

The very next day, I started planning our first true client appreciation event—months in advance, with a clear theme and plenty of lead time. We hosted a chocolate tasting. Over a hundred people came, and it was a huge success. Clients still talk about that event years later. That was when I realized something that has shaped my entire practice: clients don't remember charts or returns. They remember how you made them feel.

Financial performance may win the client, but relationship performance keeps them.

Why Events Matter More Than Returns

I've been helping clients plan their retirements since 1992, and one thing I've found is this: to be in the top tier of this business, you must know how to entertain. Numbers matter, but relationships keep people coming back. Disney taught me how to create experiences. Merrill Lynch taught me how to structure events with professionalism. When you combine the two, you create something memorable.

That's why I'm always the first one at our dinners, with drinks and appetizers waiting. At larger events, we simplify the menu so guests can quickly circle their choice. When budgets are lean, we've offered cookies with our logo instead of fancy desserts. Offering sweets sends a subtle message of appreciation—"You're sweet to us."—and it's one of those little touches clients always enjoy. I always walk clients in and walk them out. It's my way of saying I value them and their time.

> "Financial performance may win the client, but relationship performance keeps them."

I've traveled across all fifty states, attended events at Ritz-Carlton properties, Disney venues, and incredible restaurants. What I've noticed everywhere is this: the little things matter. People remember a kind word, a thoughtful detail, and the feeling of being cared for.

What Works

Arriving before anyone else sets the tone for the entire evening. Keeping things simple helps people relax. Walking clients in and out shows them I value them. And focusing on experiences, not extravagance, proves that thoughtfulness always outweighs expense. The office is where we handle investments; events are where I learn who clients really are—their hobbies, their families, their dreams. Those conversations deepen the relationship and give me the insight I need to serve them better.

Keeping things simple is another lesson I've taken to heart. At large dinners, I streamline the menu so guests can quickly circle their choice instead of flipping through endless options. That small adjustment eliminates stress, speeds up service, and lets people focus on conversation rather than logistics. The less friction they feel, the more freedom they have to enjoy the moment.

> "People talk about experiences, not spreadsheets."

I also make it a point to walk clients to their tables when they arrive and walk them out when they leave. It's a habit that says: you matter to me from start to finish. Those few extra steps are personal, memorable, and completely outside the realm of numbers or portfolios. They're reminders that this relationship is more than transactional—it's built on gratitude and respect.

One of the most common misconceptions is that great events have to be extravagant. In reality, it's the experience that sticks, not the price tag. Some of our best events happened when the budget was tight, like the year we had cookies made with our corporate logo instead of a full dessert spread. Clients loved it because it was thoughtful, creative, and unique to our firm. That's what they remembered—not how much it cost.

Finally, mixing appreciation with genuine connection is at the heart of everything I do. Conversations at events deepen relationships and give me the insight I need to serve them better.

What Successful Advisors Do Differently

I always start with a no-obligation conversation. Clients can feel the difference when there's no pressure attached. From there, I provide written investment plans that are tailored to their goals, not my product list. Every client's story is unique, so their plan should reflect their timeline, their family, and their priorities.

Consistency is another mark of trust. I don't disappear after the first meeting. We have regular check-ins—some by phone, others face-to-face, and often through events that let clients meet one another. Hosting experiences creates bonds that go far beyond business. Clients remember those moments, and they sometimes share those experiences with friends at future events.

Follow-up is non-negotiable. If a client attends an event or a meeting, I always circle back—whether it's a thank-you card, a note about something we discussed, or an invitation to continue the conversation. It shows that I was listening, and it keeps the relationship alive.

I also make it a point to serve the family, not just the individual. That means knowing the spouse, the children, and sometimes even the grandchildren. When life changes—through retirement, illness, or loss—the whole family feels it. By being present for all of them, I become more than an advisor. I measure success not by assets under management but by trust.

And in the end, I measure success in trust, not transactions. Assets under management are one metric, sure. But the real measure is whether my clients would invite me into their homes, introduce me to their children, and count on me when life gets hard. That's the business I want to be in, and that's what makes this work worth doing.

Inviting Clients and Defining Your Ideal Client

Sometimes, the smallest details make the biggest difference. A simple invitation can set the tone for an entire relationship. Imagine opening an email with the subject line: *Join Us for Good Food, Great Company, and a Little Relaxation*. The message that follows is warm and straightforward:

Hi, [First Name], we're hosting a special client evening, and I'd love for you to join us.

The details are clear—Thursday at 6:05 PM, at a familiar venue, with a casual dinner, live music, and no sales pitch. Just a night to relax, connect, and enjoy good company. The invitation closes with an open hand: *Feel free to bring a guest. We'd be honored to meet the people you care about most*. It's an easy script, but it does more than fill seats—it reinforces trust, appreciation, and genuine relationship.

Just as the right words draw clients in, the right questions help you understand who your best clients really are.

That's where the "Define Your Ideal Client" worksheet comes in. It pushes past demographics into the fears, goals, and unspoken hopes that shape financial decisions. What are clients most afraid of as they approach retirement—running out of money, losing independence, becoming a burden? What keeps them up at night—debt, market swings, family conflict? What do they hope life looks like in five, ten, or twenty years?

The conversation doesn't stop at surface answers. It digs into family roles—supporting adult children, funding grandkids' education, caring for aging parents. It makes space for hidden truths—the unspoken anxieties or the goal they've never dared to say out loud but that would light them up if achieved.

From there, the focus shifts to you as the advisor. How can your service support not just their numbers but their *why*? What conversations do you need to start so that those truths come to light? Used well, this tool helps you align recommendations with what matters most to them: security, freedom, connection, or legacy.

Together, a thoughtful invitation and a clear picture of your ideal client create a foundation for lasting relationships. One draws clients to the table. The other helps you know them well enough to serve them in the ways that matter most.

Host one relationship-focused event this quarter. Make it social, not salesy. Beforehand, write down three things you want to learn about each guest. During the event, listen more than you speak. Afterward, send a handwritten note referencing your conversation. Track how many guests bring a friend next time. That's your referral engine at work.

CHAPTER TWO

Build Your Brand Through Experience

Not long ago, we hosted an event at our local zoo. Though not the Ritz or a country club, the event became one of my most memorable gatherings to date.

A neighbor served as the zoo's marketing director, so I asked if they'd give us a discount in exchange for letting them share about volunteer opportunities and memberships. The partnership worked beautifully. Our clients loved the unique setting, the kids were entertained, and the zoo gained exposure.

The event reminded me of a truth I've seen over and over in this business: your client experience doesn't have to be lavish, it only has to be thoughtful. When clients feel

> "Clients don't stay for spreadsheets. They stay for how you make them feel."

like you've gone the extra mile to create an atmosphere of warmth, care, and intentionality, they relax. And when they relax, they share. That's when the hard work of financial advising begins.

A clear vision of your client's experience means more than your pitch. It's not simply about where you meet or what food you serve. It's about how clients feel the moment they walk in and the lasting impression they carry home.

The Toucan Touch

When I first started, I underestimated how much tone and environment shape a client's trust. Over the years, I've realized clients aren't judging your charts—they're judging how safe they feel in your presence.

That's why we developed what I call the "Toucan Touch"— our signature process for service excellence. It means clients experience consistency, care, and attention to detail every time they interact with us. They know they'll see me twice a year for a full portfolio review, they know they'll be greeted warmly at events, and they know they can count on my team to follow through on the little things.

We call it the Toucan 180° Review because every 180 days, we sit down with clients to look backward and forward. These meetings are simple, consistent, and give clients a clear picture of where things stand. By naming the process, we make it easy for clients to remember and easy for my team to deliver. You don't have to use my system, but I'd encourage you to create your own branded process that communicates consistency and care. Our Toucan 180° Review helps us know who to invite to which events. These small details lead to steady success.

What Successful Advisors Do Differently

If you know your client well, you won't need a big hotel budget to create a great client experience. All you need is intentionality.

Start with smaller gatherings that match your clients' wants and tastes—maybe a dinner for fifteen clients instead of 150—and focus on giving them at least one memorable moment. Plan your events well in advance so you can talk them up during calls and meetings throughout the year. And always follow through with gratitude, whether it's a Starbucks gift card or a short text expressing appreciation for their presence. When you align the setting, timing, and tastes with your clients' lives, your events will feel natural instead of forced.

Involve your team. Ask them for feedback or for their ideas. Check with your spouse or your kids. They often know what's popular and fun in your area. Some of our best ideas came from simply asking, "What would our clients enjoy?"

> "Your client experience doesn't have to be lavish; it only has to be thoughtful."

In my experience, successful advisors know their clients well and think about client experience the way Disney thinks about guests—every touchpoint communicates something. Here's what I've found sets the best apart.

I begin with a no-obligation invitation. Clients can feel the difference when there's no pressure to attend. When we lessen the stress, they'll tell you things they might never reveal in a sales pitch.

Consistency is critical. Follow-up is where relationships either grow or wither. After every event or meeting, I find some way to prove I listened. They spent their time. I show their investment was worthwhile to me. This keeps the relationship alive.

I measure success by whether the client seemed genuinely pleased with the experience. If they invite me to their child's soccer games or introduce me to a friend, I know I'm succeeding.

When it comes to creating a client experience vision, I remind myself of three simple truths.

First, design for delight, not simply delivery. The goal of an event isn't to tick a box or fill a room. It's leaving clients with a lasting emotional impression. Second, let the topic serve the moment. Timing matters and so does tone. A spring brunch, a fall tax talk, or a year-end vision night feels different depending on the season and the emotional needs of your clients. Third, remember that success isn't about attendance. It's about trust. From RSVP to ROI, the metric is whether relationships grew stronger.

Preparing for who will attend shapes how I plan. I see the client walking in, surveying the scene, and reacting. What are they feeling, expecting, or dreading? I paint the room, and then execute the event.

Before booking a venue or sending an invitation, I ask, What's the goal—education, connection, referrals, retention? The format follows from that answer. From there, I build in the details—invitations that reflect our tone, a clear follow-up plan, and a simple way to track what worked. The more intentional I am on the front end, the easier it is for my team to deliver an experience that feels seamless.

And while it's easy to overspend, I've found that money rarely makes the moment memorable, connections do. Sometimes that means partnering with a CPA, estate attorney, or local vendor to share costs. Seek out vendor support and speakers who will bond with your clients. Other times, it means leaning into community spaces or even hosting at a client's business. I'd rather invest in a thoughtful touch—a thank-you gift, a family photo station, a moment that feels unique—than in an extravagant spread of food. Those details are what communicate care, and care is what clients remember.

Client Experience Vision—Tone, Values, Venue

Every firm sends a message the moment a client walks through the door. Sometimes that message is intentional; sometimes it isn't. The goal of this worksheet is to make sure your message is clear, consistent, and aligned with the trust you want to build.

> "Money rarely makes the moment memorable, connections do."

Think first about tone. Ask yourself, *What do we want clients to feel when they meet with us?* Safe? Heard? Respected? Reassured? Then compare it with reality. How do clients likely feel right now, and what shifts would help close the gap? Maybe the tone you want is warm and personal, or calm and professional, or upbeat and confident. Whatever it is, name it and write down the actions that make it happen.

Next come values—the principles clients witness in the way you work. Integrity, clarity, hospitality, professionalism, transparency, service, empathy, consistency—each one shapes how people talk about your firm long after the meeting ends. Think back to stories or moments when those values showed up in action. Where are they not as visible as you'd like? Identifying gaps is the first step toward building an action plan that strengthens trust.

Finally, pay attention to the venue, the environment that clients see and step into. First impressions matter. Lighting, seating, scent, music, artwork, cleanliness, even the welcome materials on the table—all of these either reduce stress or add to it. Ask yourself, *What small changes could we make this quarter to improve the space? What could we remove to cut distractions?*

It helps to pause and imagine the one word you hope clients would use to describe their experience. Is that the word they'd use today? If not, what changes will you make to close the gap?

To keep the vision sharp, walk through your space every quarter as if you were a first-time visitor. Role-play conversations to see if tone and values come through. Write down the "tone triggers"—the words, gestures, or actions that naturally convey warmth and trust. Keep a log of positive feedback tied to the changes you make. Over time, these small intentional steps add up, turning the client experience into a reflection of your best values and the story you want your firm to tell.

Create a vision and build on your own experience. Choose one upcoming event and see it through your clients' eyes. Walk through the space, taste the food, and pay attention to the details. Ask yourself, *What message does this send? How will clients react when they walk in?* Adjust the tone, environment, and touches until the experience communicates warmth, safety, and trust.

Examine all the ways the event can go wrong and right. Plan for both experiences. Is your team's language formal, friendly, or flat? Are your core values visible—in action, not just on the wall? How do you physically signal trust, clarity, and calm? What elements of your client environment reduce stress and build emotional safety?

CHAPTER THREE

Planning Memorable Events

One of the most fun events we ever hosted was built around a theme most people wouldn't expect at a financial seminar—college.

We turned an ordinary educational session into a "529 College Night." Instead of the standard chicken dinner at a hotel ballroom, we set up a ramen bar, sliders, potato chips, and even a self-serve keg station with red solo cups. We played up the theme, and the energy in the room was completely different from a typical financial talk. That combination of education and entertainment worked. People still talk about "529 College Night" years later.

That event confirmed what I already knew but often forget: the type of event you choose shapes the experience, and the experience shapes the relationship. A forgettable dinner won't move the needle, but a well-thought-out, themed event can become part of your brand and, when done well, something others expect.

What Successful Advisors Do Differently

I've tried just about every type of client event you can imagine: small appreciation dinners, large, themed parties, webinars, golf outings, museum nights, and, as I've mentioned, even zoo events. Some worked beautifully. Others flopped. But each one taught me something valuable.

> "The type of event shapes the experience, and the experience shapes the relationship."

Educational events, for instance, work best when they're short, engaging, and wrapped in something fun. Our 529 College Night is proof of that. A dinner designed purely to thank clients—without a pitch, a presentation, or pressure—can strengthen a practice more than a dozen cold calls. Networking events serve a different purpose, creating space for clients to bring friends or connect with referral partners.

Done well, they spark a ripple effect of introductions and future opportunities.

Types of Events

Appreciation Events: The simplest yet most powerful gatherings are those with no agenda other than gratitude. A casual dinner, a holiday open house, or even an ice cream social on a hot July afternoon communicates one clear message: *We value you.* These events build goodwill that lingers far longer than any business pitch.

Educational Events: Clients want to learn, but they don't want a lecture. Educational gatherings thrive when they are concise, engaging, and paired with a touch of enjoyment. A themed dinner, a dynamic speaker, or a virtual update leaves clients with useful insights while making the time memorable.

Networking Events: These events open doors for connection, both for clients and for you. Wine tastings, golf outings, or behind-the-scenes tours are less about the content and more about creating an environment where introductions happen naturally. The relationships forged in these spaces often become the strongest.

Hybrid and Virtual Events: Sometimes the most effective way to connect is through a screen. Webinars, Zoom Q&As, or market outlook calls extend your reach, especially to those who might not attend in person. While they can't replicate the warmth of a handshake, they stretch your budget and allow access to high-profile speakers.

Signature, Small-Group, and Family Events: Beyond the basics, there are the events that define your brand—your signature gatherings. These are larger, themed occasions that clients anticipate each year, whether it's a masquerade ball, a zoo night, or a college-themed dinner. Small-group dinners are equally powerful, offering the intimacy of ten to fifteen people around a table where trust grows one conversation at a time. And then there are family events, designed to include spouses, children, and even grandchildren. A day at the ballpark or a community festival may have nothing to do with finance, but it shows that you care for the whole family, not just the portfolio.

Each of these types of events serves its own purpose. The art lies in knowing which to use and when.

Timing Matters

I learned quickly that the calendar is as important as the guest list. My first Christmas party was a failure, not because the food was bad or the invitation poorly worded but because clients were already buried in holiday obligations. That experience taught me to pay close attention to rhythm.

Seasons of Opportunity: January offers a fresh start. Clients are thinking about resolutions and money matters, which makes it an ideal time for "Year Ahead" sessions or financial outlook calls. Spring brings lighter moods and open calendars, making it perfect for brunches, garden parties, or community partnerships. Summer can be tricky—vacations and kids at home often pull families away, but casual, family-friendly gatherings work if you lean into the relaxed pace. By late August, when routines return and football hasn't yet taken over weekends, attendance soars. Fall, with its focus on year-end planning, is tailor-made for tax and estate discussions.

Daily Rhythms: Timing isn't only seasonal. Retirees often prefer daytime events when driving is easier. Younger professionals lean toward early evenings after work but before family commitments. Parents of school-aged children may find Saturday mornings more manageable than weekday nights. Knowing your clients' family makeup and lifestyle helps you choose the right moment—not just the right month.

Frequency and Cadence

In the early years, one annual event may be enough to build anticipation. As your practice grows, smaller quarterly dinners and one marquee event every other year provide balance. The goal isn't to flood the calendar but to offer just enough touchpoints that clients look forward to the next invitation rather than sigh at another obligation.

Matching Event to Purpose

Before I send an invitation, I always ask myself one question; What's the goal here? If it's education, I keep the presentation tight and add a touch of entertainment. If it's appreciation, I remove pressure and make it purely celebratory. If the purpose is networking, I design the evening for conversation and introductions. And if it's brand building, I aim for something big and memorable—a themed gala, a zoo outing, or a community partnership that sets us apart.

The right event at the right time does more than fill a room. It deepens trust and keeps your name at the top of clients' minds long after the evening ends.

Client Event Planner and Sample Scripts

Events don't succeed by accident. They succeed because every detail—from the first email invitation to the final thank-you note—is mapped out ahead of time. That's why it helps to think of planning as a journey: you begin with a clear goal, you mark the path, and you set reminders, so no step is missed along the way.

Start by naming the purpose. Is the event designed to educate? To connect? To celebrate a milestone? Once that goal is clear, the rest of the pieces fall into place. Choose the type of gathering: educational, social, or hybrid. Set the date, secure the venue, and decide on food, speakers, or co-hosts. Build in small touches—activities, gifts, or special moments—that show care and keep energy high. A simple tip saves stress later: assign every task to a person with a deadline, and rehearse or walk through the event before it begins.

Budgeting is important. Keep track of every cost—venue, food, materials, talent, gifts—and add a cushion for the unexpected. That margin protects against last-minute surprises. Follow-up deserves a spot on the plan as well. Schedule thank-you notes, event recaps, one-on-one meetings, and feedback reviews *before* the event begins so the goodwill mood in the room isn't lost afterward. The best hosts know the event isn't over until the relationships it sparked have grown stronger.

Of course, careful planning pairs best with warm communication. That's where sample scripts and templates come in. A strong subject line—"You're Invited," "Join Us," or "Let's Make a Night to Remember"—sets the tone before the first word of the invitation is read. Inside, the message is simple: here's what the event is, here's when and where it happens, and here's why it is important. There are no sales pitches, only an open door to good company and meaningful moments.

The same approach applies to printed invitations or event graphics. The words highlight connection, conversation, and community, while the details—time, date, venue, RSVP—make it easy to respond. Then, when the event begins, the host can offer a short toast that centers the guests themselves: *This gathering isn't just about a topic, it's about you. Planning is more than spreadsheets; it's found in conversations, laughter, and life shared together. Cheers.*

When you weave planning with communication, you set the stage for an event that is organized, warm, and memorable. Execution gives structure, words give heart, and together they create the kind of experience that leaves a lasting impact.

Think about your next event. Write down its primary purpose in one sentence. Then ask yourself, *What theme or format best supports that purpose?* If the goal is education, consider how to make it engaging—perhaps a themed dinner or guest speaker. If the goal is appreciation, keep it light and celebratory. Whatever you choose, match the event type to the outcome you want, and you'll see better results.

Organize a relationship-building event this quarter. In advance, list three inquiries for each guest and one personal insight for them to gain. At the event, prioritize listening over talking. Later, send a handwritten note summarizing your discussion. A few thoughtful details can elevate a one-night event into a lifelong partnership.

Chapter Four

The Execution Edge

One of the most memorable events we ever hosted was built around an Antique Roadshow brunch. We invited clients to bring a family heirloom, promising that a professional appraiser would be on hand to offer valuations and share stories. The setup was simple: coffee, mimosas, and a light brunch. But what happened that morning remains a treasured moment.

Clients showed up carrying quilts, silver trays, old watches, even a painting someone's grandfather had tucked away in a closet. As each piece was examined, the room came alive. Laughter followed when someone's "priceless" treasure turned out to be a dime-store knockoff. When a dusty vase turned out to be worth thousands, the value of the event became clear: not all our wealth is in stocks and bonds. Some might be hidden gems waiting to be found. Our Antique Roadshow brunch was entertaining, educational, and personal all at once.

That event confirmed to me that clever ideas only work if you execute them in a way that creates moments people want to retell. And when guests walk away with stories, they become your marketers.

What Works

The Antique Roadshow succeeded because people didn't just attend, they participated. They went home eager to tell neighbors and friends, "You won't believe what we found out about Grandma's china." Word-of-mouth buzz comes from designing an event with built-in stories.

Buzzworthy events share three ingredients. First, a **Story Hook**—a premise that sparks curiosity. "Bring a family heirloom." "Watch the eclipse with us at the ballpark." "Walk into a Hawaii Five-0 luau." The hook invites people into something bigger than dinner and a slideshow.

Second, a **Surprise Element**—the unexpected twist that keeps energy alive. At the Antique Roadshow, the surprise was whether a trinket was worthless or priceless. In other settings, it might be a raffle drawing, a trivia contest, or a charity box where guests suggest local causes and the group chooses one to support. Surprises keep people leaning in.

Finally, a **Shareable Finale**—the ending that makes retelling easy. It could be the winning raffle ticket, the unveiling of the top "hidden gem" restaurant from a community box, or the announcement of a charity donation. A clear arc—beginning, middle, and memorable end—gives guests a natural way to share the story. When clients leave with a story worth retelling, you've created free marketing no ad budget can buy.

> "When clients leave with a story worth retelling, you've created free marketing no ad budget can buy."

I've also seen how small touches create lift. In our Antique Roadshow brunch, a "hidden gems" treasure box gave clients the opportunity to share their favorite local spots. This idea not only sparked conversation but also helped build interest in our community. A "Charity Treasure Box" shifts the spotlight outward, as guests nominate nonprofits and the group supports one together. That single act turns an evening into something larger than ourselves.

Execution gains power when it reflects who you are. Advisors sometimes feel pressured to copy someone else's big idea, but authenticity matters more. A golf fanatic can pull off a simulator night. A music lover can weave a concert into an appreciation dinner. A foodie can partner with a local chef. Clients sense when an event fits your personality, and the buzz is stronger when it does.

What Successful Advisors Do Differently

The best advisors craft moments of surprise and delight. They think about the wow factor that makes clients say, "You won't believe what happened." It might be a Broadway performer singing in an intimate setting, a Federal Reserve Chair giving a candid talk, or something as simple as an eclipse viewed from a ballpark. Whatever form it takes, that "wow" moment becomes the hook people share over and over.

They also scale wisely. Not every event has to be big to make an impact. Our Roadshow brunch worked with twenty guests but could easily be expanded to a hundred. Smart advisors test ideas small, refine them, and then repeat the winners. That discipline makes execution repeatable instead of overwhelming.

And they pay attention to detail. From the timing of reminders to the way the room is set, details are what people notice, even subconsciously. Clients may not praise the logistics, but they remember if the event flowed smoothly. And they retell that experience as professionalism.

Above all, successful advisors design with buzz in mind. They ask, *What's the hook? Where's the surprise? How will it end?* And they build those answers into the plan.

Planning and Execution: Gaining the Edge

Every memorable event begins with a story. Not the tale told afterward, but the spark that makes people curious enough to show up in the first place. What's that hook? It might be as simple as *Bring a family heirloom*. Or as bold as *Watch the eclipse from the ballpark*. It could even be as playful as stepping straight into a Hawaii Five-0 luau.

Once the hook is set, momentum comes from surprise. A guest arrives expecting one thing then finds themselves pulled into raffle drawings, trivia contests, or even the discovery of a hidden gems box. Some hosts use a charity treasure chest where guests nominate nonprofits. However it looks, the unexpected twist keeps the energy alive.

But no event is complete without a finale. What will guests carry home and retell the next day? Maybe it's the winning raffle ticket unveiled with a cheer. Maybe it's the announcement of a donation to a local cause. Or maybe it's the reveal of the top hidden gem. The ending gives the story legs.

At each step, there's a question worth asking, *Does this plan reflect who you are?* When the event mirrors your values and personality, the buzz grows stronger.

And remember, there's no need to launch big right away. Many of the best events begin small, are refined over time, and then expand once the model proves itself. Testing before scaling keeps your practice sharp and your audience engaged.

When you weave together a story hook, a surprise element, and a shareable finale, you don't just host an event—you design a story that markets itself better than any ad ever could.

Think about your next event. Ask yourself, *What's the story people will tell afterward?* Build in one surprise moment, add one participatory element, and end with a finale that gives the evening closure and energy. When clients leave with a story worth retelling, you've created free marketing that is priceless.

Sketch out your own buzz-ready event. Start with your **Story Hook**—the premise that gets clients curious enough to show up. Add a **Surprise Element**—the twist that keeps them leaning in during the event. End with a **Shareable Finale**—the moment that makes it easy to retell afterward.

Once you've written those three, test them by asking, *Would I tell this story to a friend? Would my clients tell it to theirs?* If the answer is yes, you've got the beginnings of an event that markets itself.

Chapter Five

Follow-Up That Converts

One of the most unusual events I ever hosted came from a rare opportunity. In 2017, Columbia, South Carolina, sat in the path of a total solar eclipse. The city was filled with visitors, schools closed, and businesses adjusted their hours. Rather than see it as a disruption, we turned it into an event.

We rented a section at the local minor league ballpark and invited clients and their families to watch the eclipse with us. We provided food, drinks, protective glasses, and a little commentary on how rare the moment was. For a couple of hours, the  ballgame didn't matter. People gathered with their kids, cheered as the sky darkened, and commented when the temperature dropped.

Some clients still tell us they remember where they were—with us—when the sky went dark. More importantly, think about the impact when they talked about the event with friends, sparking interest in future invitations. The eclipse confirmed for me that anticipation is part of the experience. A great event doesn't start when the doors open; it starts weeks before, with the buzz you build.

What Works

Filling a room takes more than a single invitation. The best results come when communication is layered. Start with an initial save-the-date, followed by reminders at two weeks, three days, and even the morning of. Consistency is key. People often mean to RSVP but forget, and each reminder is a gentle nudge. Clients also become your best ambassadors when you give them the chance.

> "A great event doesn't start when the doors open; it starts weeks before, with the buzz you build."

When I personally encourage someone to "bring a friend just like you," it plants the idea that they should invite someone they respect. Those introductions are often stronger than any cold leads you could generate on your own. Scarcity plays a role too. A room that feels full creates more energy than one with empty seats. By capping attendance and making it clear that space is limited, you encourage early responses and give the event an air of exclusivity.

But good invitations are only the start. If you want your event to be bigger than the room itself, don't hope for attention—plan it so the media and community can't miss it. Reporters and social feeds follow stories with timing, visuals, and angles. If you want attention, you must give them a reason. News follows timelines, so look for ways to connect your event to a calendar milestone. When the timing answers the question "why now," you've cleared the first media hurdle.

I also think deliberately about the visuals. Cameras, whether they're held by reporters or guests, need a moment worth capturing. That means planning for a reveal, a countdown. I've found it helpful to write the hook in a single line, the way a headline might appear. "Families gather at the ballpark to watch the eclipse." "Local chef teaches families a three-course dinner on a budget." "Neighbors bring heirlooms to be appraised for charity." That discipline keeps me honest. If I can't state the angle simply, then the buzz will probably fall flat.

Once you've named the hook, share it with others. I send a simple media advisory—date, time, place, the best visuals, and who benefits—a week before and again two days prior. It doesn't need to be long; reporters prefer clarity over copy. On the guest side, I "prime" three or four clients to be ambassadors by giving them a short message they can forward—the ten-word hook, the when and where, and the RSVP line. People share what's easy to share, and when they do, your buzz grows organically.

What Successful Advisors Do Differently

Successful advisors I've observed follow the same pattern. They build events for coverage, not by chance. They tie in community partners that already have a following—arts groups, ball clubs, museums, veterans' organizations—and co-announce the event. They place two anchor moments into their run-of-show—one near the beginning, another at the end—ensuring there is always something worth posting or reporting. They also think of story prompts for guests.

I've seen advisors put small cards on tables with questions. Guests enjoy sharing their answers, and those cards become the seeds of social posts later.

Exclusivity has its place here as well. A limited RSVP window, a VIP hold-back for community partners, and a clear "this will sell out" message increase commitment. None of this requires spectacle; it requires clarity of angle, moments designed to be seen, and other people's voices placed at the center.

So how do you build this into your own planning? Start by writing the headline. If you can't tell the story in ten words, refine until you can. Next, draft a one-page media advisory. Keep it simple: the hook line, date, time, place, best visuals, and who benefits. Look at your run-of-show and plant two moments—an early reveal and a finale worth retelling. Finally, prime your ambassadors. Send each a short message they can share, and stage your social posts in the week leading up—one teasing the theme, one highlighting the partner, one promising the finale.

Do those things, and you won't just fill a room, you'll give your community a story to carry forward. That's buzz. And buzz travels farther than any single invitation ever could.

Building Buzz and Filling the Room

Imagine sitting down with your team and saying, "All right, what's our headline? Ten words or fewer that capture the heart of this event." From there, you move to the notes for a one-page media advisory. Someone at the table might say, "Let's make sure we've nailed the hook, the date and time, the visuals, and who benefits."

Next come the anchor moments. "What's the early reveal or kickoff that will draw people in?" someone asks. Another voice chimes in, "And what about the finale—the surprise or announcement that sends everyone home talking?" Then you discuss ambassadors. "Who are the people we can reach out to personally who will help amplify this?"

The second part shifts to sparking conversation in the room itself. Picture a host placing small cards at each table. A guest picks one up and reads, "What's a place you've always wanted to visit and why?" Another card prompts, "Who was your favorite teacher when you were growing up?" Someone else asks, "What book, movie, or show have you recommended more than once?"

The questions keep moving. "What food reminds you most of home?" "What's a skill you've always admired in others?" "If you could invite anyone from history to dinner, who would it be?" Soon, the cards are sparking laughter, reflection, and stories.

As the evening winds down, you hear more: "What small daily habit makes your life better?" "What song always lifts your mood?" "What's something you learned the hard way but are glad you know now?" "What's a local spot where you love to spend a quiet afternoon?"

By the end, the cards have done their work. Guests have shared stories, swapped memories, and left with conversations still lingering—exactly what makes an event both memorable and worth sharing.

Look ahead on your calendar. What's a moment you can build anticipation around? It might be a community event, a seasonal milestone, or something unique to your city.

Once you've chosen, sketch your communication plan. Write down when you'll send your first invitation, when you'll follow up, and how you'll keep the buzz alive in between. Then, identify three clients who could serve as ambassadors—people you can personally invite to bring a friend "just like them."

Finally, plan your scarcity. Decide on your cap for attendance and how you'll word the invitation to reflect that space is limited. Scarcity creates energy, and energy fills rooms.

Chapter Six

Failures, Flops, and Fixes

Not every story ends the way you expect it to.

One night, we hosted a private showing of *The Bucket List*. The idea was simple: gather clients, serve popcorn and snacks, and enjoy a film that touched on meaning and legacy. Halfway through, a client's phone rang with devastating news—his wife's grandmother had passed suddenly, and she left in tears. The room fell silent. It changed the entire event, and there was not a dry eye in the theater.

In that moment, the event wasn't about a movie anymore. It was about compassion, presence, and letting everyone know we cared—for the sister, yes, but also for the group. We pivoted to what mattered most: people. There was no need to finish the film. We all knew the story and its ending. That sudden interruption, tragic as it was, said more about valuing time and relationships than Morgan Freeman and Jack Nicholson ever could.

Another evening, at a dinner event, a client enjoyed a little too much wine. When he stood to leave, he stumbled and nearly fell. Everyone saw it. How we handled that moment mattered more than the menu, the décor, or the presentation. With a distraction, we pivoted away from his embarrassment and redirected the group's attention elsewhere. Then quietly, we helped him exit, made sure he got home safely, and carried on.

The lesson stuck with me: the true measure of professionalism isn't whether everything goes right but how you respond when things go wrong.

What Works

I've seen how the smallest details can steady an event when surprises hit. Guests don't expect perfection, but they do notice how you treat them in difficult moments. I've studied how to build margin into the agenda so that if something goes sideways—traffic delays, bad weather, or a guest needing extra care—we're not scrambling, complaining, or blaming.

Tone-setting matters too. Events stay safer and more enjoyable when you avoid divisive topics and give clients room to enjoy one another. Some of the best conversations happen when you create space instead of programming every moment. Flexibility creates room for laughter, connection, and even awkward moments to find their rhythm.

Preparation means planning for backup. Outdoor event? Always check the forecast and secure an indoor option. Transportation snag? Keep a rideshare number handy. Tech failure? Have a low-tech solution ready. These aren't dramatic fixes, but they show forethought, and clients remember that.

What Successful Advisors Do Differently

The advisors I admire most don't panic when disruptions occur. They move to plan B or C without drawing attention to the pivot. They respond with calm professionalism. They seat like-minded clients together so conversation flows. They greet every guest, make introductions, and close with gratitude.

> "The true measure of professionalism isn't whether everything goes right but how you respond when things go wrong."

I've also seen great advisors brief their teams with what-ifs ahead of time: What if the speaker is late? What if a guest overindulges? What if the power goes out? When the unexpected happens, everyone is caught off guard.

More than anything, successful advisors remember that events are about people, not programs. A movie cut short by tragedy isn't a failure if the client feels loved. A dinner disrupted by a stumble isn't ruined if the guest was shown care and respect. Handling disruptions with grace often leaves a stronger impression than when everything runs without a hitch.

Prepare for the Unexpected Companion Reflection

Before your next event, pause for a moment and imagine what might go wrong. Picture the rain that could drive your guests indoors, the traffic jam that could delay arrivals, the microphone that might refuse to work, or even the awkward moment when a client says something off-color. Then, before the day arrives, walk yourself through how you would respond. Do the same with your team. Say out loud, "If this happens, here's what we'll do." That simple rehearsal ensures no one freezes when the unexpected arrives.

Next, consider the atmosphere you want to create. Are there topics that could divide the room? How might you gently redirect a tense conversation back to warmth? Think of it as setting a current. Once the flow is established, guests naturally drift along with it.

And finally, look at your schedule. Is there any breathing room? An agenda with no margins is fragile. But an agenda with space allows you to absorb delays, handle interruptions, and still make guests feel cared for.

CHAPTER SEVEN

Scaling Your Strategy

For the smallest event I ever hosted, we rented time on a golf swing simulator. Nothing fancy, just eight clients, a coach, and a screen that froze each swing in midair. About an hour in, one client waved me over and said, "I brought two buddies. They're better golfers than I am, but they could use your help more than I do." We laughed, but I paid attention. Those two friends were at an inflection point—one changing jobs, one navigating a complex rollover for his dad. None of that came up in the room. It emerged a week later when I followed up.

That night taught me something we should never forget: the event is the spark, and the **follow-up is the fire**. People remember how they felt, but they act when you help them carry the moment forward.

What Works

I've settled into a simple cadence that turns good nights into durable outcomes. Within **24 hours**, I reach out personally. No mass note, just a short message that names a specific moment from the evening. "I'm still thinking about your draw-fade," or "I loved hearing the story about your dad's first set of clubs." Two lines, human and specific.

Within **72 hours**, my team and I send a concise recap: one highlight, one resource promised, and one next step that costs nothing: an article, a checklist, or an introduction we volunteered to make. The point is to keep the momentum without making it transactional.

By **day 7**, we close the loops we opened. If I said I'd introduce two guests who hit it off, I do it then—brief, gracious, and permission-based. "You two mentioned volunteering with youth sports; here's a quick intro so you can compare notes." If someone raised a planning question we didn't unpack at the simulator, I offer a short call—not a pitch, just a way to finish the conversation we started.

At **30 days**, we check in on anything that was in motion. Not a sales cycle, more like a neighborly "How did that go?" And around **90 days**, we invite people back into something small and relevant—a coffee, a micro workshop, or a seat at a table where they'll meet two people they'll genuinely like.

The mechanics matter, but the **substance** matters more. Our notes capture three things the night of the event: who a guest brought, one thing that delighted them, and one thing they're working on (career, family, estate, health). We log those details where they belong and train ourselves to use them. There's no magic, only the discipline of noticing, recording, and returning.

Follow-up lands best when it extends the event's value *without asking for anything*. If we featured a hidden gems in the community box at a dinner,

> "The event is the spark, but the follow-up is the fire."

the follow-up includes the compiled list—cleaned up, mapped, and easy to share. If the group chose a charity, our message includes the donation confirmation—made by us, on behalf of everyone who attended—plus a short story about the impact that gift will have. If a speaker offers a framework, we send a one-page version guests can use with their families. People appreciate being part of something that outlasts an evening.

What Successful Advisors Do Differently

The best advisors I know design their follow-up with the same care they put into the event. They mentally **segment** the room afterward—clients, prospects, first-timers, and those who brought a friend—and tailor next steps accordingly. A first-timer might get a warm "hope you felt welcome" note and an easy on-ramp: "If you'd like the retirement checklist we mentioned, reply 'checklist' and we'll send it." A guest with a friend deserves specific gratitude that honors the trust implicit in bringing someone to the event. A prospect who asks a technical question receives a short, clear answer and an offer to dig deeper with no pressure attached. Clients need to know we appreciate their loyalty and value the relationship.

The best advisors also **connect people to each other**. If two guests find common ground, they affirm the common connection—a simple, respectful reintroduction with one line explaining how they know each other will suffice. Those bridges do quiet work, building goodwill and widening the circle that supports your clients when you're not in the room.

On the operational side, the best advisors treat each event like a coach. A quick **next-morning huddle** while memories are fresh captures what worked and what didn't.

A more in-depth **72-hour debriefing** logs costs, note-taking quality, timing friction, and surprises. A **30-day look back** measures movement—new introductions, scheduled reviews, families reengaged, and the handful of conversations that turned into planning work.

> "Events create moments, but the follow-up turns moments into relationships."

None of those meetings are long. They are simply consistent and measure the right things.

Attendance is a variable; **introductions lead to stability**. A full room feels good; **retention and trust** pay the bills. The advisors who grow from events know their ratios: invitation to RSVP, RSVP to arrival, arrival to meaningful conversation, meaningful conversation to next step. They watch those over twelve to twenty-four months because events compound. The simulator night that leads to a plan review today may become a multigenerational relationship a year from now. That is your horizon.

Finally, they close the loop **publicly but with humility**. A short note to all attendees thanking them for their attendance, questions, comments, and suggestions makes them the hero, not you. When other people shine, you bask in their glory.

Follow-Up and Lasting Impact

Before your next event, build a 24-7-30-90 plan and put names to it.

Within 48 hours, send one personal message to each attendee that mentions something only they would recognize, plus a short recap that delivers a promised resource.

By day 7, complete every introduction you offered, and invite any open questions to a short call.

At day 30, check on outcomes you set in motion; if a guest asked for a tool, confirm they received and used it.

Around day 90, extend one relevant invitation—small, specific, and generous.

Create a simple **Event Ledger** you'll use every time: a single page with four columns: Name, Who They Brought, What Delighted Them, What They're Working On. After each event, fill it in and act on it. Then pick **one** community artifact you can send to everyone—the curated list you assembled, the charity's thank-you note, or a one-page tool that makes their life easier. Let the evening prove it wasn't a moment; it was the start of something durable.

The simulator night ended with a hug in the parking lot and a quiet promise: "I'll follow up." We did. In similar situations, guests have later chosen to become clients or introduce family members after thoughtful follow-up. It's not the technology or the venue that makes the difference—it's the care, clarity, and consistency that carry the night forward. That's the work of follow-up, where events become relationships, and relationships build the lasting foundation of a practice.

Appendix

Event Scripts: Check-In Greeting & Welcome Toast

These scripts provide a warm, professional framework for welcoming guests and setting the tone. Adapt them to your voice while keeping the focus on guest comfort and connection.

Greeting Guests at Check-In

Welcome! We're so glad you're here.

[Smile warmly, offer a handshake if appropriate]

Hi [Guest's Name], thank you for coming tonight. Please check in here and feel free to grab a drink or mingle until we begin.

If this is your first time joining us, we're thrilled to have you. There's no presentation right away—just a chance to relax and connect. Let me know if you need anything at all!

Pro Tip: Assign a team member as "Guest Radar" to notice and engage anyone alone or looking unsure.

Welcome Toast

Good [evening/afternoon], everyone.

Thank you for being here—it truly means the world to us. Tonight is about you: your goals, your story, your future.

Whether we've known each other for years or this is your first event, we hope this space feels welcoming, thoughtful, and inspiring.

So here's to good company, great conversations, and all that lies ahead—cheers!

Pro Tip: Memorize your opening and closing lines for a confident delivery.

Variations & Enhancements

- Personalize the greeting by referencing how you met or a recent conversation.
- Mention a highlight or special element of the evening to build anticipation.
- Thank any co-hosts, partners, or sponsors at the start to acknowledge their support.

Companion Worksheet

This worksheet accompanies Chapter Five: **Building Buzz and Filling the Room.** It includes two things: a guide for planning media-friendly events and prompts for table conversations.

Part One: Event Buzz Planning

Use this section to plan your event for coverage, not chance. Write your headline, prepare your advisory, and outline two anchor moments.

Event Headline (ten words or fewer):

One-Page Media Advisory Notes (hook, date/time, visuals, who benefits):

Anchor Moment 1 (early reveal or kickoff):

Anchor Moment 2 (finale, surprise, or announcement):

Ambassadors to Prime (names and outreach notes):

Part Two: Conversation Starter Prompts

- What's a place you've always wanted to visit and why?
- Who was your favorite teacher growing up?
- What's a book, movie, or show you've recommended to friends more than once?
- What food reminds you most of home?
- What's a skill you've always admired in others?
- Who in history would you invite to dinner if you could?
- What's a small daily habit that makes your life better?
- What song always lifts your mood?
- What's something you learned the hard way but are glad you know now?
- What's a local spot where you love to spend a quiet afternoon?

Print these prompts on small cards and place them at tables during your event. Encourage guests to pick one and share their answer. These questions invite laughter, reflection, and connection—the kind of conversations that make events memorable and shareable.

Prepare for the Unexpected Worksheet

This worksheet accompanies Chapter Six: **Prepare for the Unexpected.** Use it to anticipate possible disruptions, plan calm responses, and ensure your team is ready to handle curveballs gracefully.

What-If Planner

List five potential challenges and outline how you would respond to each. Share this with your team before the event.

Potential Challenge	Planned Response

Tone & Connection

What topics or activities should you avoid to keep the atmosphere safe and welcoming? What can you do to encourage natural, warm conversation instead?

Breathing Room

Where in your agenda can you add margin so small disruptions don't throw off the flow?

Clients don't expect perfection. They expect presence, care, and calm leadership. Use this worksheet to prepare for the unexpected and show your professionalism when it matters most.

Client Event Planner: From Idea to Impact

This enhanced planner takes you from initial concept to post-event follow-up with a focus on creating experiences that strengthen relationships, generate referrals, and showcase your brand's care.

Pre-Event Planning

Goal: What's the purpose of this event? Select one or more:

- ☐ Educate
- ☐ Connect
- ☐ Generate referrals
- ☐ Celebrate a milestone
- ☐ Other: _____

Event Type:

- ☐ Educational
- ☐ Social
- ☐ Hybrid

Theme or Topic: _____

Audience:

☐ Existing Clients
☐ Prospective Clients
☐ Multi generational Families
☐ Other: _____

Event Details:

- Date & Time: _____

- Venue: _____

- Speakers / Co-hosts: _____

- Food / Drink: _____

- Activities or Special Touches: _____

Tasks & Timeline

Tip: Assign every task a clear owner and deadline to avoid last-minute stress.

Add rehearsal/walkthrough dates to ensure readiness.

Task	Responsible Party	Due Date	Completed (✓)
Book venue			
Confirm speakers/co-hosts			
Design invitations			
Send invitations			
Prepare handouts/materials			
Confirm RSVP count			
Finalize menu/logistics			
Print name tags/table cards			
Prepare thank-you gifts			

Budget Tracker

Tip: Include a 10% contingency fund for unexpected costs.

Item	Estimated Cost	Actual Cost	Notes
Venue Rental			
Food & Beverages			
Speaker/Talent			
Printing/Materials			
Gifts or Giveaways			
Decorations/Setup			
Miscellaneous			
Total			

Follow-Up Plan

Tip: Schedule follow-up actions before the event begins so they're not forgotten.

Action	Responsible Party	Due Date	Completed (✓)
Send thank-you notes			
Email event recap/photos			
Schedule 1:1 follow-ups with attendees			
Add notes to CRM			
Log feedback/suggestions			
Evaluate event ROI/emotional impact			

Pro Tips for Success

- Partner with other professionals to share costs and expand reach.
- Include interactive elements to keep guests engaged.
- Document the event with photos/videos for future marketing.
- Track not just attendance but referrals and follow-up meetings generated.

Client Experience—Sample Email Invitation

Below is a refined and customizable email invitation template you can use to invite clients to relationship-focused events. It feels warm, personal, and engaging while allowing for quick edits to suit the tone, formality, and specifics of your event.

Subject Line Ideas

Choose one that matches your event's mood:

- An Evening Just for You—Join Us for Great Food & Company
- Celebrate With Us: Good Friends, Great Conversations
- You're Invited—Let's Share a Memorable Evening Together

Email Body Template

Hi [First Name],

We're hosting a special client evening, and I'd love for you to join us. This is our way of saying thank you for being such an important part of our community.

When: [Day of Week], [Date] at [Time]

Where: [Venue Name & Address]

What to Expect: [Brief description—e.g., "A casual dinner, live music, and a chance to connect with old friends and meet new ones."] There will be no presentations and no sales pitches—just an evening to relax, enjoy, and connect.

We would be honored to meet the people you care about most if you bring a guest.

Please RSVP by [RSVP Date] by replying to this email or calling [Phone Number]. If you have any dietary preferences or accessibility needs, please let us know so we can make sure you're comfortable.

Looking forward to seeing you there!

Warmly,

Michael
[Your Firm Name]
[Contact Info]

Pro Tips for Maximizing RSVPs

- Send the email at least 3–4 weeks in advance, with a reminder one week before the event.
- Use a subject line that hints at exclusivity or personalization.
- Add a personal sentence or two at the top if you have a recent touchpoint with the client.
- Include a photo from a past event in the email body to make it more engaging.
- Consider including a link to a calendar invite to make adding the event easier.

Client Experience Vision Worksheet—Tone, Values, Venue

This expanded worksheet helps your team define and align every aspect of the client experience. It goes beyond surface-level impressions to address tone, values, and environment in a way that reinforces trust, loyalty, and emotional connection. Use it during leadership meetings, team retreats, or annual reviews to ensure your firm's client experience vision is intentional and consistent.

1. Tone—What Clients Feel

When a client walks in, I want them to feel:

- ☐ Safe
- ☐ Heard
- ☐ Understood
- ☐ Respected
- ☐ Reassured
- ☐ Other: _____

Our ideal tone during client meetings is:

- ☐ Warm and personal
- ☐ Calm and professional
- ☐ Upbeat and confident
- ☐ Gentle and clear
- ☐ Other: _____

How we currently make clients feel: _____
Tone shifts we need to make: _____
Actions to achieve the shift: _____

2. Values—What Clients Witness

Core values we want clients to experience (check all that apply):

- ☐ Integrity
- ☐ Clarity
- ☐ Hospitality
- ☐ Professionalism
- ☐ Transparency
- ☐ Service
- ☐ Empathy
- ☐ Consistency
- ☐ Other: _____

Stories or moments that best reflected our values in action:
_____

Areas where our values are not showing up clearly enough:
_____

Action plan to address gaps: _____

3. Venue—What Clients See

First impressions when someone walks into our space:
_____

Physical elements that currently support a calm, professional vibe:

- ☐ Lighting
- ☐ Layout and seating
- ☐ Scent / music
- ☐ Cleanliness
- ☐ Artwork or visuals
- ☐ Welcome materials (beverages, folders, signage)
- ☐ Other: _____

Small changes we could make this quarter: _____

What could we remove to reduce stress or distraction?
_____

Final Reflection

If a client were to describe their entire experience in one word, we hope they would say: _____

What word might they say now? _____

What will we change to close that gap? _____

Pro Tips for Implementation

- Conduct a quarterly walk-through of your client experience as if you were a first-time visitor.
- Role-play client scenarios to test how tone and values show up in conversations.
- Document your firm's "tone triggers"—words, gestures, or actions that convey warmth and trust.
- Keep a log of positive client feedback tied to tone, values, and venue changes.

Define Your Ideal Client's "Real-Life" Fears & Goals

This worksheet is designed to help you go beyond demographics and uncover the emotional, practical, and aspirational drivers behind your ideal client's financial decisions. Use it with your team, during client interviews, or as part of your onboarding process. The goal is to gain a deep, empathetic understanding that informs how you serve, communicate, and build lasting relationships.

Step 1: Emotional Drivers

What is your client most afraid of as they approach retirement? Why does this fear matter to them?

Probe deeper: Is the fear related to running out of money, losing independence, or becoming a burden to family?

Notes: _____

What keeps them up at night when it comes to money?

Consider both tangible (debt, market volatility) and intangible (family conflict, job insecurity) worries.

Notes: _____

Step 2: Aspirational Goals

What do they hope life looks like in 5, 10, or 20 years?

Ask about lifestyle, travel, family, work, hobbies, and legacy aspirations.

Notes: _____

What role does family play in their financial decisions?

Are they supporting adult children, funding grandkids' education, or caring for aging parents?

Notes: _____

Step 3: Hidden Truths

Are there unspoken anxieties (health, legacy, lifestyle) that might affect their planning?

Use open-ended questions to create a safe space for sharing.

Notes: _____

What goal have they never said out loud—but would light them up if they achieved it?

Listen for moments of excitement or emotion when they talk about the future.

Notes: _____

Step 4: Advisor Actions

How can your service support those emotional or life-centered goals?

Align recommendations to their "why," not just their "what."

Notes: _____

What conversations do you need to initiate to uncover these truths?

List specific topics, stories, or questions you'll use to draw out deeper insights.

Notes: _____

Pro Tips for Using This Worksheet

- Revisit this worksheet annually for each client. Priorities and fears shift over time.
- Use active listening—repeat back what you've heard to confirm accuracy.
- Share observations gently to help clients articulate what they may not have been able to say before.
- Involve family members when appropriate for a more complete picture.

Event-Day Logistics: Run-of-Show Checklist

This enhanced Run-of-Show checklist ensures your event flows seamlessly, from setup to guest departures. It allows you to assign responsibilities, confirm timing, and prepare for contingencies so you can handle surprises with confidence.

Pre-Event Preparation

- Conduct a complete A/V check and test backup equipment.
- Walk the venue as a guest would to identify gaps in signage, flow, or comfort.
- Rehearse greetings, introductions, and transitions with your team.
- Confirm catering, signage, and printed materials are ready.
- Ensure hospitality items (water, name tags, coat rack) are in place.

Run-of-Show

Time Slot	Activity	Responsible Party	Status (✓)	Contingency Notes
3:00 PM	Venue Setup / A/V Check			Backup mic, spare batteries, extra extension cords
4:30 PM	Final RSVP Confirmations			Adjust seating/table count
5:00 PM	Guest Arrival / Check-In			Assign greeters at entrance
5:15 PM	Welcome Remarks / Toast			Have printed notes ready
5:30 PM	Main Presentation / Activity			Assign timekeeper
6:30 PM	Q&A or Client Conversations			Prepare 2–3 discussion prompts
7:00 PM	Thank-You Gift Distribution			Ensure extras available
7:15 PM	Guest Departures			Assign staff to farewells
7:30 PM	Cleanup & Debrief			Capture feedback for the next event

Post-Event Follow-Up

- Send thank-you notes or emails within 48 hours.
- Log feedback and suggestions for future events.
- Follow up with attendees who brought guests for potential introductions.
- Share event highlights in your newsletter or on social media.

Event Debrief & Salvage Plan Worksheet

Use this expanded worksheet to conduct a thorough post-event analysis when things don't go as planned. The goal is not only to identify what went wrong but also to extract lessons, take corrective action, and actively rebuild trust and momentum with clients.

Step 1: What Happened?

- Briefly describe the event and what went wrong. Be factual, not emotional.
- Include details such as timing issues, technical failures, guest experience gaps, or communication breakdowns.

Example: "The A/V system failed ten minutes before the keynote, causing a delayed start and reduced speaking time."

Step 2: What Did You Learn?

- What surprised you during the event?
- What early signs did you miss or ignore that could have prevented the issue?
- Did you underestimate a risk you could have prepared for?

Example: "We relied on the venue's A/V without a backup mic. A pre-event technical check would have caught the problem."

Step 3: How Did You React?

- How did you respond in the moment: calmly, defensively, or reactively?
- What did your team see and hear from you during the crisis?
- Did your actions reassure guests or add to their discomfort?

Example: "We stayed calm, acknowledged the delay, and offered refreshments while the issue was fixed."

Step 4: What Would You Do Differently?

- What specific steps can you take next time to prevent the same problem?
- Is there a person, vendor, or process that needs to change?
- How can you add redundancy to critical event elements?

Example: "Hire a dedicated A/V tech, have two microphones, and build a fifteen-minute buffer into the schedule."

Step 5: What's Your Salvage Plan?

+ Who needs a follow-up call, apology, or personal note?
+ Can you send a recap, thank-you, or new invitation that restores goodwill?
+ Is there a way to reframe the flop into a learning opportunity or shared laugh?

Example: "Send attendees a link to the recorded keynote along with a discount for the next event."

Step 6: Long-Term Improvements

+ Add this incident to your "Lessons Learned" file for future training.
+ Update checklists, run-of-show documents, and contingency plans based on this experience.
+ Conduct a team debrief to ensure everyone understands the changes going forward.

Pro Tips for Salvaging Client Trust

+ Own the problem quickly and directly—avoid excuses.
+ Communicate the fix before the client wonders if there is one.
+ Offer something tangible to offset the inconvenience (bonus content, personal meeting, or special invite).
+ Follow up twice—once immediately and again after changes are implemented.

Event Scaling Blueprint Worksheet

Use this expanded blueprint to evaluate your last event and identify opportunities to scale without increasing your workload. The aim is to delegate effectively, automate smartly, capture key moments, and repurpose content so your reach grows even when your time doesn't.

Step 1: What Should You Delegate?

- List every task you personally handled that could be trained out to another person.
- Identify who on your team or in your network could take ownership with the right guidance.
- Consider outsourcing tasks like graphic design, photography, or technical setup.

Example: "Name tag creation can be handled by an assistant with a simple template."

Step 2: What Can You Automate?

- Review your RSVP process—can registration, reminders, or confirmations be automated via event software or CRM?

- Automate post-event follow-ups using prewritten templates customized for each attendee.
- Use calendar scheduling tools to eliminate manual back-and-forth for post-event meetings.

Example: "Set up an automated 'Thank You for Attending' email with a link to event photos."

Step 3: What Should You Capture?

- Decide ahead of time what you want recorded—speaker sound bites, group shots, candid networking moments.
- Capture quotes from attendees for future testimonials.
- Record short video clips for social media reels or highlight videos.

Example: "Film the room during applause to convey energy in future promotions."

Step 4: What Can Be Repurposed?

- Reuse slides, handouts, or interactive exercises in future events or webinars.
- Turn key takeaways into social media posts, blog articles, or email newsletters.
- Extract audio clips for podcast use or learning modules.

Example: "Convert a live Q&A into a blog post titled 'Top 5 Questions from Our Clients.'"

Step 5: What's Your Next Scalable Move?

- Could you offer a virtual or hybrid version to broaden attendance?
- Could a partner or sponsor extend your reach without additional workload?
- Is there a smaller, repeatable format you could run more frequently with less effort?

Example: "Turn the annual gala into quarterly micro events run by junior advisors."

Pro Tips for Scaling Without Losing Quality

- Document your event process so others can replicate it without guesswork.
- Train your team to make decisions in your absence—trust is key to scale.
- Keep a "content bank" of reusable photos, templates, and scripts.
- After each event, ask yourself, "If I weren't here, what would break?" Then fix that gap.

Event-Day Logistics: Run-of-Show Checklist

Use this template to keep your event running smoothly from setup to sendoff. Assign responsibilities, confirm timing, and ensure nothing slips through the cracks.

Time Slot	Activity	Responsible Party	Status (✓)
3:00 PM	Venue Setup / A/V Check		
4:30 PM	Final RSVP Confirmations		
5:00 PM	Guest Arrival / Check-In		
5:15 PM	Welcome Remarks / Toast		
5:30 PM	Main Presentation / Activity		
6:30 PM	Q&A or Client Conversations		
7:00 PM	Thank-You Gift Distribution		
7:15 PM	Guest Departures		
7:30 PM	Cleanup & Debrief Notes		

Follow-Up Touchpoint Tracker

This expanded tracker ensures consistent, intentional follow-up after every client event. The goal is to transform goodwill from the event into trust, referrals, and ongoing conversations.

Client & Event Info

Client Name: _____

Event Attended: _____

Notes from Event (interests, personal details, follow-up ideas):

_____

Touch One: Thank-You
- Type: Email or handwritten note
- Goal: Reinforce personal connection and express genuine appreciation

Date Sent: _____ | Notes: _____

Touch Two: Thoughtful Nudge
+ Type: Article, podcast, resource, or event-specific takeaway
+ Goal: Add value based on their interests or conversation points from the event

Date Sent: _____ | Resource: _____

Touch Three: Invitation Forward
+ Type: Coffee, review meeting, next event invitation
+ Goal: Keep the relationship moving forward and deepen trust

Date Offered: _____ | Response: _____

Follow-Up Completion
All touches completed: ☐ Yes ☐ No
Conversion Outcome: _____

Referral Potential Identified: ☐ Yes ☐ No | Details: _____

Pro Tips for Using This Tracker
+ Complete as much detail as possible during the event while memory is fresh.
+ Always personalize the thank-you—reference something specific you discussed.
+ Schedule follow-up tasks in your CRM to avoid missed opportunities.

Signature Events

Here are a few of my favorite events. Each one is distinct and fun-oriented.

Please ensure compliance approval before promoting or hosting.

2025

- **Jan 15:** *The Year Ahead in the Market* (Zoom)—Market outlook for 2025

2024

- **Aug 17:** *Antique Roadshow*—Talks on financial market themes and valuing family heirlooms
- **Jan 20:** *2024 Market Outlook Chili Zoom* (Zoom)

2023

- **Jan 22:** *The Year Ahead in the Market*—Guest speaker Jeremy Schwartz

2022

- **Sep 16:** *Pre UGA vs. USC Happy Hour & Educational Event*
- **Mar 29:** *Russia–Ukraine Market Update* (Zoom)
- **Jan 22:** *Raising the Bar* (Zoom)

2021

- **Sep 12:** *The Red Bandanna*—Tribute to 9/11 hero Welles Crowther
- **Jun 17:** *In the Room with Leslie Odom Jr.* (Zoom)
- **Mar 18:** *In the Room with Dr. Ben Bernanke* (Zoom)
- **Jan 23:** *2021 Market Outlook Webinar*—With Jeremy Schwartz

2020

- **Nov 11:** *10 Truths No Matter Who Wins*—Post-election insights
- **Oct 16:** *Hawaii Five-O Luau Walk-Through*—City Roots
- **Jul 15:** *Speaking of Markets*—With T. Rowe Price
- **May 27:** *Managing Retirement Income*—With Thornburg
- **May 9:** *Fidelity Market Outlook*—With Fidelity Investments
- **Apr 22:** *Managing Stress Amid COVID-19*

- **Mar 31:** *COVID-19 Contraction*—Investment outlook
- **Jan 25:** *2020 Market Outlook Webinar*—With JP Morgan

A Beginner's Guide

As I said, as you begin this journey, you may be in a situation where you have an extremely limited budget, are brand new, or are just starting out. Some things you might want to think about in the early days include co-sponsoring with an attorney, CPA firm, or other top professional in your area.

So how do you get good ideas for events? If you're naturally creative, the process may come easily. If not, borrow creativity from those around you. Ask your spouse, your team, even your children what they're excited about. Reach out to your referral partners, your centers of influence, and your clients. Ask questions. What's happening on these dates? What are people doing in your community? In many markets, college sports are a big deal. Right now, pickleball seems to be everywhere. In some communities, urban activities and downtown experiences are very popular. Any of these can be a great place to start. Most importantly, do what fits you. I'm not much of a wine aficionado, so I've hesitated to host wine tastings because it wouldn't feel sincere for me. The best ideas grow out of who you are and what you genuinely enjoy.

One of the most effective techniques is to cap attendance. Set a firm limit on how many people can attend and communicate that clearly. When you talk with clients, you can honestly say, "We only have room for X people at this event, so please register early so we can save you a seat." That simple cap creates a healthy sense of urgency. When clients bring guests, treat that as a transfer of trust. Send a text, email, or handwritten thank-you note to the client and, when appropriate, to the guest. Let them know you appreciate the introduction. Learn what makes the guest tick, enter that information into your follow-up system, and send a recording or summary of the event afterward.

Here are some examples to consider: go to the finest car dealership and arrange a car test. Another great idea for client entertainment is to go to your favorite car mechanic and host a session for new and retired drivers on car maintenance.

In addition, many libraries and retirement communities offer programming that you can tag along with. If you have a local retirement center, they often have a host of speakers, events, and projects that you can partner with in the early days until you build up your budget.

Consider partnering with other professionals. If you have referral partners that you work with, share your resources—or consider partnering with another financial advisor within your office. There are ways to think outside the box.

In the early days, you'll have a limited budget. Later, you'll have to stay within that budget, and once your rate of return improves, you'll have more flexibility. But remember, it's not a quick solution. Guests might attend your events and not do business for six months—or even two years. That's why you need a great marketing pipeline and follow-up system.

When guests attend your event, make sure you're reaching out and following up with them. Have a procedure—whether drip email, drip marketing, LinkedIn, Facebook, or social media—to keep your name top of mind.

You don't have to start off with a Ritz-Carlton or Mercedes-Benz budget. You may want to start with a ham-and-cheese budget to get things going. It's the authenticity and the thought that you care that matter. It's not the dollar amount invested—it's the heart and passion behind it.

Where to Begin

A great place to start is your administrative team. Ask them what they think and get their feedback. Check with home office staff, business coaches, and expert partners to learn what others in your area are doing.

Reach out and talk with clients about their interests. Set a trial date. Start small. See how it goes and take notes. Get input from your team and advisory board, then evolve.

You won't start off doing events for 150 people right out of the gate. Start with fifteen, see how it goes, then build to twenty, thirty, fifty, and so on. Depending on your brand, business, and support staff, you'll determine the next step.

It's a gradual evolution. In the early days, start small, build momentum, and go from there. I like to have the next event planned out a year in advance so that, over the course of the year, every phone call, email, and client meeting can promote the next event. That helps keep the momentum going.

Event Timing and Strategy

In January, we like to host an event that sets the tone for the year ahead. It's more of an educational or marketing event—less entertainment—but it all ties together.

We've found that inviting larger firms or well-known speakers to come to our local area works well. It's easier to arrange visits with vendors you already work with. Check their resources—you may be surprised at the relationships they have with large financial service companies, annuity providers, and third-party managers.

In the past, we used to fight the weather at the start of the year, but we found it easier to do these events via Zoom. We schedule our more social events later in the year.

To be honest, we try to wrap up by football season. Football plays a big part of life in the South, and we don't want to compete with the ACC or SEC. When we do fall events, we hold them during the week. I prefer Saturdays—it's quieter and allows us to focus on people.

These are just some tidbits to think about as you kick off your financial services entertainment success.

Contact Information

For more information about Michael Oana, please text, email: christine@michaeloana.com or call 803-790-8989.

We are available to speak at your next event—team or regional—by phone, Zoom, or in person.

We love to travel, and I have been to all 50 states. Follow along by visiting our website at michaeloana.com, as well as on LinkedIn and Facebook.

Past Presentations

We have presented *The Recipe* to

- Merrill Lynch
- Summit Brokerage Services
- The Columbia CEOA Association
- Cetera Shark Tank National Team Meeting
- Cetera Peer-to-Peer National Conference

...to name a few, along with countless one-on-one mentoring sessions.

About the Author

Certified Retirement Counselor®

Michael Oana is the founder of Michael Oana Retirement Planning Specialists in Columbia, SC. His team helps clients plan and implement investment strategies for Columbia's corporate managers.

Michael graduated from the University of South Carolina Moore School of Business in 1992 in 3 ½ years with a BS in Marketing and a second degree, a BS in Management.

The Moore School of Business is consistently ranked as the #1 international business school in the United States.

Michael earned a "Duckturate" Degree during his college internship at Walt Disney World.

After graduation, Michael spent 13 years with Merrill Lynch, rising up the corporate ladder from an unpaid apprentice to an assistant vice president. He retired from the corporate jungle in 2005 to create his own boutique investment firm, Michael Oana Retirement Planning Specialists.

He holds Series 7, 24, 63, and 65 Securities registrations and is registered in about twenty-two states, in addition to holding an insurance license in South Carolina.

After completing the Cetera Wealth Management course at the University of Texas and Georgia Tech Executive Education Center, Michael received the Certified Retirement Counselor Designation in 2018.

Michael served on the Cetera Advisors National Conference and Marketing Committee. In 2019, he presented at the Connect 2019 Conference and was awarded the Summit Financial Group MVP Award. This is given to the advisor who makes the most contributions to the firm.

To see more great pictures of our events, please visit our website: www.michaeloana.com.

Michael has been featured in the *Star Paper*, *The State Paper*, and *Columbia Metropolitan Magazine* and has been interviewed on WIS TV and numerous radio stations about the benefits of retirement planning.

In 2019, as part of the Cetera National Connect Convention, he was interviewed on *Good Morning Columbia*, along with being featured on a podcast with Amy Adams.

Active in the community, he is the founder of the Columbia CEO Association and has served on several top non profit boards, such as the Columbia Chamber of Commerce Business Expo Committee, the Columbia Classical Ballet, the Columbia Affordable Housing League, and the Rosewood Elementary Foundation, where he was a member and the President for two years.

To help tourism and give back to the local community, he designed, created, and led the Hootie and the Blowfish Street renaming project in Five Points. The night of the street renaming, over 5,000 fans attended the event and tribute concert. Craig Melvin of *The Today Show* was the host of the event.

Mr. Oana is married to Heather, and they have two wonderful sons, London and Lane. They reside in Shandon, and he attends and is a former trustee at Shandon Presbyterian Church. He has a passion for faith, family, and football and has been to all 50 states. He, last but not least, has a pet, Coco, who is a chocolate cockapoo, and they share a love of walks and snacks.

The Financial Advisor's Guide to Building Trust

How One Superfan Made Hootie a Permanent Fixture in Columbia

Michael Oana, a longtime Hootie & the Blowfish fan, was the driving force behind the creation of both the Hootie & the Blowfish monument and the naming of a street in their honor in Columbia's Five Points district. Inspired by a dream over a decade earlier, Michael set out to thank the band for their positive impact on the city and their role as ambassadors of Columbia.

He initiated and led the effort, forming a committee, coordinating design plans, and overseeing the two-year process from concept to completion. While he originally envisioned a "Mount Rushmore of Hootie," the final design reflected a more artistic tribute agreed upon by the group. Through his persistence and community spirit, Michael helped create a lasting landmark celebrating the band's legacy and their roots in Five Points—an area Darius Rucker once called "the center of his universe."

Today, the monument and street stand as iconic symbols of Columbia's musical history, thanks largely to Michael Oana's vision, dedication, and gratitude toward a band that helped put his hometown on the map.

Speaker Promo Sheet

Michael Oana
Michael Oana Retirement Planning Specialists
Certified Retirement Counselor® | Founder, Michael Oana Retirement Planning Specialists
4408 FOREST DR
SUITE 2001
COLUMBIA, SC 29206

Columbia, SC | 📞 803-790-8989 | 🌐 MichaelOana.com

Keynote Speaker | Workshop Leader | Advisor Mentor

Michael Oana helps financial professionals grow their practice by creating memorable client experiences. With 30+ years in financial services and insights gained from Disney and Merrill Lynch, Michael equips advisors to build trust and encourage introductions—one event at a time.

Most Requested Topics

1. Entertain to Retain
How to build lasting client relationships through strategic events

2. The Experience Factor
Lessons from Disney, Chick-fil-A, and the Ritz for financial advisors

3. Turn Appreciation into Acquisition
Using events to create opportunities for introductions without being pushy

What Attendees Will Learn, Gain, and Produce

- Why clients stay loyal to advisors who show appreciation
- What types of events work for different audiences and budgets
- How to follow up after events to create opportunities for referrals
- How to turn entertainment into a repeatable system

Ideal For

- Financial Advisor Conferences
- Brokerage Teams & Regional Offices
- Advisor Training Workshops
- Client Appreciation Programs

Previous Speaking Venues

- Merrill Lynch
- Cetera Shark Tank Team Meeting
- Columbia CEO Association
- Summit Brokerage
- National Peer-to-Peer Conferences

My Thanks

My thanks to the many folks who love and support me.

Super special to my parents and steps, family, and the starters, Heather, Lane, London, plus Coco and my Disney "Brothers."

My work family for calming me down and restricting my Diet Mt Dew intake, and my love, Heather, for agreeing to be my wife and partner, 100% in writing.

PS. No in-laws were harmed in the making of this guide, and thanks for letting the Founder have so much fun over the years.

Our Mission Statement

As **Retirement Planning Specialists**, we love helping our clients plan and implement their retirement dreams—whether that means a retirement full of travel, friends, or family.

We take great pride in being the **financial advisor of choice**.

We measure daily success in handshakes and hugs, and we strive to shift the burden of worry away from our clients. Our education, training, hard work, and teamwork allow us to serve others while providing for our own families.

www.ingramcontent.com/pod-product-compliance
Lightning Source LLC
LaVergne TN
LVHW061037070526
838201LV00073B/5083